The Bacharach and David Song Book

by *Burt Bacharach*
and *Hal David*

Music edited by Norman Monath
With an Introduction by Dionne Warwick

Simon and Schuster ☐ New York

Sole selling agent of this edition: Simon and Schuster
Rockefeller Center, 630 Fifth Avenue, New York, N.Y. 10020

THIRD PRINTING

SBN 671-20494-7
Library of Congress Catalog Card Number: 70-116496
Designed by *Libra Studios, Inc.*
Music autographing by *Maxwell Weaner*
Manufactured in the United States of America

Contents

Introduction

I t's hard for me to talk about Burt Bacharach and Hal David without talking about myself as well, because to me we're a team and the three of us belong together. Each has his own job to do. Hal's is lyrics, Burt's is music, mine is singing. If you respond to the lyrics Hal writes and the music Burt composes, you already know what kind of men they are: honest, imaginative, full of emotion. But I have an inside view of them I want to share with you. Good friends are those you want to be with as much as possible. Every time you're together, you learn about each other. Things you like and respect. As the friendship grows, you want others to meet them, enjoy their company, share your good fortune in knowing them. I'm not only talking about Burt and Hal. I'm also talking about the songs they have written. These men and their songs have been the very best friends I have ever had. They have made me aware of the beauty of the world as well as the heartaches—helped me to know how to handle both extremes of living. They have helped me to grow up in my understanding of myself and others.

T heir songs have a life and personality of their own. Just as Hal and Burt do, they respond to my laughter and my sorrow, they share my hopes and my frustrations. They soften the hard bumps and help lift my joy higher than I could manage alone.

Hal and Burt don't write especially for me. It just feels that way. When I do something of theirs it becomes mine, I make it mine. I know what they're trying to say and what they are saying. We have worked together so much and so closely, and we understand and like each other so well, that I automatically fall into the slot that's already grooved. It's like mental telepathy. We're on the same wavelength, wanting to say the same things about life and the living of it.

In a way I feel very much a part of these songs and the two men that make them. These two are very dear to me. That's why I can't help feeling that although there have been great recordings of their songs by other singers—and terrific singers too—I somehow come closest to interpreting them. When I'm recording their songs I am recording *me*.

DIONNE WARWICK

What the World Needs Now Is Love

love,   No, not just for some, ____ but for ev - 'ry - one. ____

Lord, we don't need an - oth - er moun - tain, ____
Lord, we don't need an - oth - er mead - ow, ____

There   are   moun - tains   and   hill - sides   e -
There   are   corn - fields   and   wheat fields   e -

nough to   climb; _____   There   are   o - ceans   and
nough to   grow; _____   There   are   sun - beams   and

Anyone Who Had a Heart

ALFIE

Very slowly, rubato

What's it all a - bout, Al - fie? Is it just for the mo - ment we live? What's it all a - bout when you sort it out, Al - fie?

From the Paramount picture *Alfie*

sure   as I be - lieve   there's a heav - en a -

bove,   Al - fie,   I know   there's some - thing much

more.   Some - thing e - ven non - be - liev - ers can be - lievc in.

I be - lieve in love,   Al - fie.___   With - out true love we just ex -

17

ist, Al - fie. Un - til you find the love you've

missed you're noth - ing, Al - fie. When you walk let your heart

lead the way and you'll find love an - y day,

Al - fie, Al - fie.

Blue on Blue

1. I walk a - long the street we used to walk. Two by
   lone - ly night we meet in dreams. As I

two lov - ers pass and as they're pass - ing by
run to your side you wait with o - pen arms;

I could die 'cause you're not here with me.
o - pen arms that now are closed to me.

Now the trees are bare, there's sad - ness in the air and
Through a vale of tears your vi - sion dis - ap - pears and

I'm as blue as I can be. Blue on blue, heart-ache on heart-ache,
I'm as blue as I can be.

blue on blue now that we are through. Blue on blue,

heart-ache on heart-ache and I find I can't _____ get o-ver

los-ing you.   2. Night aft-er los-ing you. _____

21

DON'T MAKE ME OVER

Slow rock tempo

Don't make me o - ver ___ Now that I'd do an - y - thing for you. Don't make me o - ver ___ Now that you know how I a - dore you. Don't pick on the things I say, ___ The things I do. ___ Just love me with

all my faults___ the way that I love you.___ I'm beg - gin' you.___

Don't make me o - ver ___ Now that I can't make it with -

out you. Don't make me o - ver.___ I would - n't change one thing a -

bout you. Just take me in - side your arms___ and hold me tight ___ and al - ways be

Ac - cept me for the things I _ do. _

Ac - cept me for what I am, _

Ac - cept me for the things I _ do. _

Keep repeating and fade out

Ac - cept me for what I am, _____

Ac - cept me for the things I _ do. _

The Windows of the World

Moderato, not too fast, lightly relaxed

The

Win - dows of the world are cov - ered with rain.
Win - dows of the world are cov - ered with rain.
Win - dows of the world are cov - ered with rain.
Win - dows of the world are cov - ered with rain.

The
The
The

28

A HOUSE IS NOT A HOME

Slowly and expressively

A chair is still a chair _____ e - ven when there's no one

sit - ting there; But a chair is not a house, and a

From the Embassy picture *A House Is Not a Home*
Copyright © 1964 by Joseph E. Levine Music Corp.

house is not a home when there's no one there _____ to hold you tight, and no one there you can kiss good - night. A room is still a room _____ e - ven when there's noth - ing there but gloom; But a room is not a house, and a house is not a home when the

two of us ___ are far a - part and one of us has a bro - ken

heart. Now and then I call your name and

sud - den - ly your face ap - pears; ___ But it's just ___ a cra - zy game ___

___ when it ends it ends in tears Dar - ling, have a heart, ___

31

way you smiled at me. *(Whistle _____)* I'd

like the world to know *(Whistle)* the sto - ry of my life, *(Whistle)* the

mo - ment when your lips met mine, and that first ex - cit - ing time I

held you close to me. *(Whistle _____)* The

sor - row when our love was break - ing up, the mem-'ry of a bro - ken

heart.___ Then lat - er on the joy of mak - ing up,

nev - er, nev - er more to part.___ There's one thing left to

do be - fore my sto - ry's through.

(Whistle)   (Whistle)

Boy: I've got to take you

Girl: You've got to take me

for my wife
for your wife so the sto-ry of my life can start and

end with you. Some end and

start and end and start and end with

(Whistle _____)
you.

8va

The Man Who Shot Liberty Valance

The kind of a man the west would need to tame a trou-bled land; _____ 'Cause the
When noth- ing she said could keep her man from go- in' out to fight. _____ From the

point of a gun _____ was the on-ly law _____ that Lib-er-ty un-der-stood. _____ When it
mo-ment a girl _____ gets to be full grown_ the ver-y first thing she learns _____ when two

came to shoot - in' straight and fast _____ he was might-y good.
men go out _____ to face each oth - er _____ on-ly one re - turns.

Man - y a man would face his gun and man-y a man would
Ev- 'ry -one heard two shots ring out, one shot made Lib- er- ty

fall, _____ The man who shot Lib-er-ty Val-ance, he shot
fall, _____ The man who shot Lib-er-ty Val-ance, he shot

Lib-er-ty Val-ance, he was the brav-est of them all. _____
Lib-er-ty Val-ance, he was the

2. The love of a brav - est

of _____ them all. _____

WIVES AND LOVERS
(Hey, Little Girl)

Moderately, not too slowly

Hey, lit-tle girl, comb your hair, fix your make-up, soon he will o-pen the

door. _____ Don't think be-cause there's a ring on your fin-ger

you need-n't try an-y-more. _____ For wives should al-ways

From the Paramount picture *Wives and Lovers*
Copyright © 1963 by Famous Music Corporation

You may not see him a - gain, _____ for wives should al - ways be lov - ers too Run to his arms ___ the mo - ment he ___ comes home to you. He's al - most here. _____ Hey, lit - tle girl, bet - ter wear some- thing pret - ty, some - thing you'd

wear to go to the cit - y; And dim all the lights, pour the

wine, start the mu - sic, time to get read - y for

love. _____ Oh, time to get read - y, time to get

read - y, time to get read - y for love. _____

WHAT'S NEW, PUSSYCAT?

Moderate waltz tempo

C **F⁶** **G⁶** **Dm C**

What's new pus-sy-cat whoa _____ What's new

F⁶ **G⁶** **Dm C** **D D⁷**

pus-sy-cat whoa _____ oh. _____

Chorus

G **B♭**

1. Pus-sy-cat, pus-sy-cat, I've got flow-ers and lots of hours ___ to
2. Pus-sy-cat, pus-sy-cat, you're so thrill-ing and I'm so will-ing to
3. Pus-sy-cat, pus-sy-cat, you're de-li-cious and if my wish-es can

spend with you   So go and pow-der your cute lit-tle pus-sy-cat nose._
care for you   So go and make up your big lit-tle pus-sy-cat eyes._
all come true   I'll soon be kiss-ing your sweet lit-tle pus-sy-cat lips._

Pus - sy-cat, pus-sy - cat, I love you
Pus - sy-cat, pus-sy - cat, I love you
Pus - sy-cat, pus-sy - cat, I love you

yes I do._____ You and your pus-sy-cat nose._
yes I do._____ You and your pus-sy-cat eyes._
yes I do._____ You and your pus-sy-cat lips._

What's new pus-sy-cat whoa_____

Trains and Boats and Planes

I'm wait-ing here like I prom-ised to.___ I'm wait-ing here, but where are you?

Fade out 2nd time

Trains and boats and planes ___ took you a - way, ___ but ev - 'ry time ___

___ I see ___ them I pray, ___ and if my prayers ___ can cross the sea, ___ the trains and the

boats and planes _____ will bring you back, back home to me. ___

50

WALK ON BY

With a beat

1. If you see me walk-in' down the street and I start to cry ___ each time we meet,
2. I just can't get o - ver los-in' you and so if I seem ___ bro - ken and blue, ___

Walk on by, ___   Walk on by. ___

Make be - lieve ___ that you don't see the tears, Just let me grieve ___ in
Fool - ish pride, ___ that's all that I have left, So let me hide ___ the

pri - vate, 'Cause each time I see you, I break down and cry.
tears and the sad - ness you gave me when you said good - bye.

Walk on by,___ Don't stop, Walk on by.___

Don't stop, Walk on by.___

Only Love Can Break a Heart

Moderately slow

mp

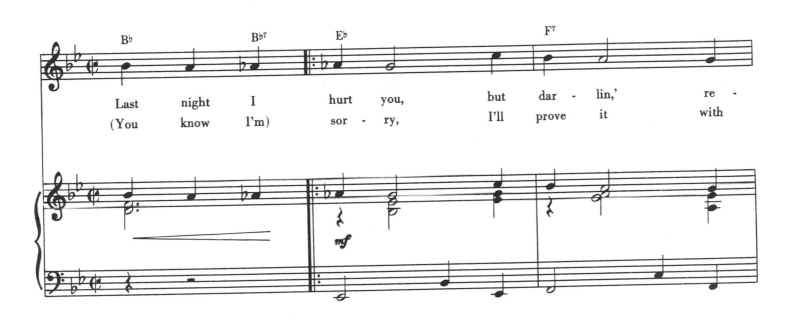

Last night I hurt you, but dar - lin,' re -
(You know I'm) sor - ry, I'll prove it with

mf

mem - ber this, On - ly love can
just one kiss, On - ly love can

Twenty-four Hours from Tulsa

56

one day a-way_ from your arms._____ I saw a wel-com-ing light and
one day a-way_ from your arms._____ She took me to_ the ca-fé I

stopped to rest_ for the night,___ and that is
stay she said O-kay Oh I was

on-ly____ twen-ty-four hours from Tul-sa_____ on-ly___ one day a-way_from your
on-ly____ twen-ty-four hours from Tul-sa_____ on-ly___ one day a-way_from your

arms._____ The juke-box start-ed to play and night-time turned_ in-to
arms._____ I hate to do_ this to you but I love some-bod-y

to Coda

MY LITTLE RED BOOK
(All I Do Is Talk About You)

I just got out my lit - tle red book the min - ute that you
No girl who's in my lit - tle red book just ev - er could re -

said good - bye _____   I thumbed right
place your love _____   And each girl

From the Charles K. Feldman Production *What's New, Pussycat?*
Copyright © 1965 by United Artists Music Co., Inc.

thru my lit - tle red book I was - n't gon - na sit and cry _____
in my lit - tle red book knows you're the one I'm think - ing of _____

_____ And I went from A to Z.
_____ Won't you please come back to me.

I took out ev - 'ry pret - ty girl in town _____ They
With - out your pre - cious love I can't go on _____ Where

danced with me and while I held them
can you be I need you so much

ANY OLD TIME OF THE DAY

arms   still need you so. And e - ven though you walked out of my   life,   you are my life. ___

___ You are my love   for   al - - - - - - - - - - - - - - - -

ways.   An - y old time of the day,   you know __ that you can

call me. __ I'll be   there, __ just   wait - ing __ for   you.

(There's) Always Something There to Remind Me

1. I walk a - long the cit - y streets you used to
2. When shad - ows fall I pass the small ca - fé where
3. If you should find you miss the sweet and ten - der

walk a - long____ with me; ____ And ev - 'ry
we would dance____ at night; ____ And I can't
love we used ____ to share; ____ Just come back

71

step   I take re - calls   how   much ___   in   love   we   used ___   to   be. ___
help   re - call - ing   how   it   felt ___   to   kiss   and   hold ___   you   tight. ___
to   the plac - es   where   we   used ___   to   go   and   I'll ___   be   there. ___

___   Oh,   how   can   I   for - get   you, _____

When there is   al - ways   some - thing there ___   to   re - mind   me;

Al - ways   some - thing there ___   to   re - mind   me.

I was born to love you _____ And I will
nev - er be free, You'll al - ways be a part of me. _____ Wo __ wo __

1. 2.
wo. _____

3.
wo. _____

Repeat ad lib. — fading out

I'll nev - er love an - oth - er, ba - by. __
I nev - er will for - get you, ba - by. __
You'll al - ways be a part of me, oh. __

A MESSAGE TO MICHAEL
(Also known as "A Message to Martha")

You'll Never Get to Heaven
(If You Break My Heart)

78

Chorus:

look - ing _____ at you. _____ You'll
an - gels _____ would cry. _____ You'll
an - gels _____ will see. _____ You'll

Nev - er get to heav - en if you

break my heart.___ So be ver - y care - ful not ___ to make ___ us part.

You won't get to heav - en if you ___ break my ___ heart, ___ Oh no,

no. _____

Keep repeating and fade out

dim. poco a poco

They Don't Give Medals
(To Yesterday's Heroes)

You should have been there when I was twen-ty,___ You nev-er heard such ap-plause,___ But now I'm twen-ty-five___ and hard-ly an-y-one___ knows I'm a-live,_____ But there's no use in look-in' back,___ be-cause:

Moderately (a tempo)
CHORUS:

They don't give ___ med-als ___ to yes-ter-day's he-roes, 'Cause
I mean to ___ bor-row ___ one day from to-mor-row, And

yes-ter-day's o-ver ___ and I've got to live ___ for to-
I'm gon-na spend it ___ on sun-shine and things ___ that I

day. I'm go-in' plac-es and no-thing can
love. I'm gon-na reach out and touch ev-'ry

stand in my way. Yes-ter-day is o-ver, No, they don't
star up a-bove. Yes-ter-day is o-ver, No, they don't

81

give med - als   to   yes - ter-day's   he - roes,   I   know   my
give med - als   to   yes - ter-day's   he - roes,___   so   wrap   up   that

way   now,   I'll   nev - er   look   back   from   this   day___   on.___
lov - in'   cup,   I'm   a   win - ner   from   this   day___

on. _____   Yes - ter - day   is   o - ver,   Can't   you   see

it's   o - ver,   And   I   be - gin   liv - in'   to - day.

poco e poco rit. e dim.

HERE I AM

Here I am, here I'll stay, All of my life we'll be to-geth-er from now on. I was a-fraid but now my doubts and fears have gone, Here I

83

keep my arms wound a-round you _____ for-ev-er. Here I am, here I'll
stay, All of my life I'll be what you want me to be, All that I ask is that you just keep lov-ing me, Here I am _____ and here I'll al-ways stay. Close to you, _____ in love _ with you, my dear. Close to

Keep repeating and fade

rit.

85

Make It Easy on Yourself

I SAY A LITTLE PRAYER

While comb - ing my hair now
At work __ I just take time

and won - d'ring what
and all __ through my

dress to wear now _____
cof - fee break time _____

I say a lit - tle prayer for you. __
I say a lit - tle prayer for you. __

Excitedly

For - ev - er, for - ev - er you'll stay in my heart __ and

I will love you for - ev - er and ev - er. We nev - er will part. __ Oh,

how I'll love you. To - geth - er, to - geth - er, that's how it must be. To

live with - out you would on - ly mean heart - break for me.

me. My dar - ling, be - lieve me,

for me there is no one but

Reach Out for Me

hold him   and kiss him   and love him   and show him that you care.   Show him that you

care   just for him, ___   Do the things ___   he likes to do, ___   Wear your hair ___

___   just for him ___   'cause ___   You won't get him   think-in' and a-pray-in', ___

wish-in'   and a-hop-in'. ___   'Cause wish-in'   and hop-in'   and think-in'   and pray-in',

98

Are You There
(With Another Girl)?

Oh, I'm stand - ing on your door - step and I don't know what to do.___
Oh, I on - ly know I love you and I could - n't say good - bye.___

Should I ring your door - bell or just walk a - way? My friends all say___ that you were nev - er
So if there's an - oth - er I don't want to know.. If you should go,___ oh, I would sure - ly

true.
die.

Hid - ing in the shad - ows

Love re - quires___ faith. I've got___

___ a lot of faith, but I hear the mu - sic com - in' out of your ra - di - o.___

(Oom - pah - pah pit - y the girl. __)

(Oom - pah - pah pit - y the girl. __

__) Oh, I on - ly know I love you and I could - n't say good - bye. __

So, if there's an - oth - er I don't want to know. __ If you should go, __ oh, I would sure - ly

die. You would nev - er leave me, hurt __ me or de - ceive me. I'm a fool to doubt you, wor-

ry so a-bout you. Love re-quires faith. I've got a lot of faith, but

I hear the mu-sic com-in' out of your ra - di o. (Oom - pah-pah pit-y the girl.

(Oom - pah-pah pit-y the girl.) (Oom - pah-pah pit-y the girl.

dim.   poco   a   poco   rall.

MAGIC MOMENTS

Slow shuffle

1. I'll nev - er for - get the mo - ment we kissed the night of the hay - ride,
2. The tel - e - phone call that tied up the line for hours and hours,
3. The way that we cheered when - ev - er our team was scor - ing a touch - down,
4. The pen - ny ar - cade, the games that we played, the fun and the priz - es,

the way that we hugged to try to keep warm while tak - ing a sleigh - ride;
the Sat - ur - day dance {I/you} got up the nerve to send {you/me} some flow - ers;
the time that the floor fell out of {my/your} car when {I/you} put the clutch down;
the Hal - low - een Hop when ev - 'ry - one came in fun - ny dis - guis - es;

Refrain

Mag - ic mo - ments, mem - 'ries we've been

I Just Don't Know What to Do with Myself

know what to do.___ Like a sum-mer rose

needs the sun and rain, I need___ your

sweet love to ease all the pain.

I just don't know what to do with my-self. Don't know

Do You Know the Way to San Jose?

109

and pump - ing gas.___
and ride___ a way.___

I've got lots of

friends in San___ Jo - se.

Do you know the

way to San___ Jo - se?

Can't wait to get back to San___ Jo - se.

Keep repeating and fade

dim. poco a poco

8va

This Guy's in Love with You

Moderately slow, with a light beat

You see ___ this guy, ___ this guy's in love with you. ___

Yes, I'm ___ in love. ___ Who looks at you the way I do? ___

When you smile, ___ I can tell we know each oth-er ver-ry well. How

PROMISES, PROMISES

With fire

mf

G   A(G)   F#m⁷   C   D(C)

Prom - is - es, prom - is - es, I'm all through with prom - is - es, prom - is - es,
Prom - is - es, prom - is - es, this is where those prom - is - es, prom - is - es,

Bm⁷   Am⁷   Am⁷

now! I don't know how I got the nerve ___
end! I won't pre - tend that what was wrong ___

D¹¹   G maj⁷   C maj⁷   F maj⁷ (add ⁶)

___ to walk out. ___ If I shout, ___ re - mem - ber
___ can be right. ___ Ev - 'ry night ___ I'll sleep now,

From the Broadway musical *Promises, Promises*
Copyright © 1968 by Blue Seas Music, Inc., and Jac Music Company, Inc.
A publication of Edwin H. Morris & Company, Inc., by arrangement with the copyright owners.

Whoever You Are, I Love You

Faith - ful and warm, when I'm in your arms, and then, when you leave, _____ you're
Some - one I know as the man I love, or the man I wish _____ I

so un - true.}
nev - er knew.}
But how - ev - er you are, _____ Deep down what-

ev - er you are, _____ Who - ev - er you are, _____ I love you.

Some-times your eyes look blue to me.

I'll Never Fall in Love Again

I'll nev-er fall in love a-gain. ___

1. What do you get when you kiss a {guy, — / girl, —} You get e-nough germs to catch___
2. What do you get when you give your heart, You get it all bro-ken up___
optional: 3. What do you get when you need a {girl, — / guy, —} You get e-nough tears to fill___

___ pneu-mo - nia, Aft - er you do, she'll nev - er phone___ you;
___ and bat-tered, That's what you get, a heart that's shat - tered;
___ an o - cean, That's what you get for your de - vo - tion;

I'll nev-er fall in love a - gain. ___

Raindrops Keep Fallin' on My Head

From the 20th Century-Fox film *Butch Cassidy and the Sundance Kid*
Copyright © 1969 by Blue Seas Music Co., Inc., Jac Music Co. and Twentieth Century Music Corp.

I said I did - n't like the way he got things done. Sleep - in' on the job. Those

rain - drops are fall - in' on my head. They keep fall - in'! But there's one thing I know,

The blues — they send — to meet — me won't de - feat —

— me. It won't be long — till hap - pi - ness — steps up